BEAUTY
FOR ASHES

Keishandra Smith

ISBN 979-8-88751-956-2 (paperback)
ISBN 979-8-88751-957-9 (digital)

Copyright © 2023 by Keishandra Smith

All rights reserved. No part of this publication may be reproduced, distributed, or transmitted in any form or by any means, including photocopying, recording, or other electronic or mechanical methods without the prior written permission of the publisher. For permission requests, solicit the publisher via the address below.

Christian Faith Publishing
832 Park Avenue
Meadville, PA 16335
www.christianfaithpublishing.com

Jeremiah 29:11 "For I know the thoughts that I think towards you, saith the Lord, thoughts of peace, and not of evil, to give you an expected end. (KJV)

Proverbs 14:12 "There is a way that seemeth right unto a man, but the end thereof are the ways of death" (KJV)

Isaiah 43:19 "Be alert, be present. I'm about to do something brand-new. It's bursting out! Don't you see it? There it is! I'm making a road through the desert, rivers in the badlands. (MSG)

Isaiah 61:3 "To console those who mourn in Zion, To give them beauty for ashes, The oil of joy for mourning, The garment of praise for the spirit of heaviness;

Printed in the United States of America

CONTENTS

Chapter 1: It's Not about the Outward. It's about What's Underneath 1

Chapter 2: Identity 8

Chapter 3: Pride 12

Chapter 4: Forgiveness 16

Chapter 5: What You Do Today Will Affect Your Tomorrow 22

Chapter 6: It Takes Two, but It Starts with One 36

Chapter 7: Comfort Zone 43

Chapter 8: Beauty for Ashes 49

I WOULD LIKE to first thank God for allowing me to write this book. Through the years, God has taken me through many journeys to bring this to fruition. Thank you for always being there and never letting me give up, even when I wanted to. You've seen everything about me and have always seen me when others couldn't. Thank you for writing my story.

Mike, thank you for allowing God to use you to bless my life in many different ways. We've been on this journey for a long time, and it has definitely been one to remember! Thank you for giving our children something I've never had. I love you. To my six beautiful children, I love you, and as I always say, "Do your best and let God do the rest." Continue to *SMIILE* always!

To my mother, you always knew that I had more in me than what I thought, and although we didn't always see eye to eye and there were a lot of things that I didn't understand, now I do. I also learned later in life that you have *always* been my *biggest* support system. I wouldn't be where I am today if it wasn't for your love and support. I love you.

To Daddy, your ability to hold a conversation is unmatched. LOL. I love you.

To my family, the Smiths and Edwards, thank you for always supporting me and loving me authentically. I love y'all.

Last but not least, Coach Sophia Ruffin. Thank you for creating a safe space for writers like me. Thank you for the push and the help to make me hold myself accountable. The support you've shown has been amazing and has definitely been a prayer answered. Thank you.

To all my readers,

    I hope that this book inspires, motivates, and builds strength and faith by the time you're finished reading it. May this be a door opened for you to walk into the healing that God has waiting for your specific needs.

    In life, we see many beautiful things, but are they really as beautiful as we see them? Is it an outward thing? Or is it authentically beautiful? When we say things like "That was beautiful" or "She's beautiful," what do we really mean? Have you ever thought about the elements that make things beautiful? Take a moment and think about some of the things that we call beautiful or incorporate the word *beauty* with.

    Are they surface things only? Or do they go deeper than that? Are they concrete or superficial? I've been on both sides of the word *beautiful*—giving the compliment and receiving it as well.

    How deeply do we hold the term *beauty*? Beauty is only skin deep.

    I grew up a happy child and was born a happy baby—that's what my mother would always tell me. I didn't really start to hear people use words like *pretty*, *beautiful*, etc. until I was much older. Growing up in the bay area, I had a decent childhood, I had friends, and I was involved in many extracurricular activities. Although my mother worked at night and things were tough for us, she did her best to support me in the best possible way she could.

    However, as I got older, things started to shift—shift in a way I never expected. I was about sixteen years old when I started to see another side to my mother that I'd never known. The insecurities that my mother possessed showed. As I watched my mother and the way our relationship shifted, I began to shift as well but didn't know it. However…

She used to always have a frown on her face, and nobody knew why except her and God. In front of me, she would say things about herself that would hurt me, and this hurt me because I never looked at my mother in the same light that she looked at herself in. I looked at her as my hero—my mother! She was the strongest woman I knew and the example that I trusted.

I knew she wasn't perfect, but I knew she wasn't those things that she said about herself either. I used to think, *How could she think like that? Where was this coming from?* And I wished she would stop saying those things. These were my thoughts. I didn't start to encourage her until I felt like I had the strength and the ability to, which was when I was older.

Even in my older years, I would still have to hear my mother tear herself down, and it left me feeling alone without an example in a few areas, not to mention having to watch the difficult events take place for her. I needed my mom. I wanted my mom, but I used to feel helpless to see hidden parts that needed a healing surface. Where was the beauty?

There were many times in my life when I thought I wasn't as beautiful as the next person. Even though I would get compliments a lot over the years and even today, I still didn't feel beautiful like people would project me to be. Why was that? What did they mean by *beautiful*?

At times, I felt that if my skin was a few shades lighter, if my personality was different, if my hair had a different texture, or if I dressed differently, then I'd fit into the crowds that I admired the most (outward things). There were certain crowds that favored young ladies who fit the description that I'd just named.

I began to feel insecure as time went on, and without me knowing it, it started to affect me. Insecurity can be a dangerous thing if it's not dealt with at the root. It can start to trickle over into other areas of your life if you're not careful. It can tear away at you internally, and ashes start to form from all the burning. It's interesting that I grew up in the church and still managed to have these issues and more. One would think that I would've been around enough strength, confidence, and resources to provide the buildup that was needed.

In life, we experience many things that cause hurt, pain, insecurity, brokenness, and so much more. These things are hard to deal with, and well, there are a lot of us who are just outright afraid to deal with them. There are times that we think that if we ignore it, then we'll be okay because we don't have to face the very thing that's killing us.

God tells us in his Word in Isaiah 61:3 that he'll give us *beauty* for ashes, the oil of *joy* for mourning, and the garment of *praise* for the spirit of heaviness. I know we can all reflect on times past and, even now, see areas of our lives where we've had ashiness, and I'm not talking about skin; I'm talking about times we've suffered from mourning and dealt with heaviness. I had a problem facing the thing that was killing me, and it turned into something else.

My insecurity continued to grow along with other things that latched on, and then I got into a relationship at nineteen years old. My first serious one. Being insecure and being in a relationship are *two* of the *worst* possible things together. Little did I know that it would be all a part of God's plan. I mean, I had experienced a part of life that touched me in a way that I thought would be too good to be true.

I didn't know how insecure I was until much later, because I had such a young mind, of course, that I thought if the right relationship came around, all my problems would be solved. If I got with the one right guy, the desire of having love in my life would be settled. As I started to explore the relationship world, I soon began to see that it was not as simple as I thought it would be. I've had guys diss me because I wouldn't give up my pearls. Why give up something precious to me when I know that you don't care about me at all?

Another reason was the Bible. I've always had that conviction about premarital sex. I still managed to try to fit in. Oddly enough, I even had friends who were doing just the opposite but still always encouraged me to stand strong like I was.

So when what I thought was the perfect relationship came around, I was tested like never before! I'm trying to live righteously, but yet in love. Kinda hard to manage sometimes, ya know? I thought I had things in order. I thought my life was going to go one way until God showed me differently. Was it hard to accept? Absolutely!

I finally felt whole and like I was worth something to a guy. These are the effects of missing out on my father's love, but little did I know that God would show me real love. I was looking for true love in all the wrong places.

Things eventually burned up, but *God* got tremendous glory out of it because souls were saved! God used us to bring many people to him and have their lives changed from the inside out. How *awesome* is that! I had no idea that God would use that as the beginning of my ministry.

However, after that is when the real ashes began. I eventually learned how to let God perform his Word in my life, and because of that, he gave me real beauty for ashes. What are some things in your life that God can turn into beauty from your ashes? I never thought beauty could come out of anything that I've been through. I used to think I would only be damaged goods.

In this book, you will read about trials, tribulations, and triumphs. You will see how God can take all the ugly things that are hidden, turn them into ashes, and give beauty to them. Whether it be an abuse of any kind, emotional instability, or a lack of love, just to name a few. As I share my story of how I got on the road to healing, I hope that you apply what's needed so that you can do the same.

Will you let God give you beauty for your ashes?

It's Not about the Outward. It's about What's Underneath

FROM A CHILD, we grow up with many different ideas or figures of what we want to or should be like. We are all born in sin, and as we get older, we (as the Bible tells us) are shaped in iniquity. Thank you, Pastor Adam and Prophetess Eve (just kidding)! Iniquity is a hidden sin. Things that are hidden in our hearts are one of the many things that can and will keep blocking our relationship with God.

Iniquity comes in all forms. When I was growing up, I had so many things that I identified with, and they helped *shape* me. I tried to find my identity in those different things without realizing it, and as I got older, I started to have iniquity and didn't know it. The more I began to go through tests and trials and development in my walk with Christ, these things started to be revealed to me. It started with insecurity.

I grew up in a household where my relationship with God and education were very important, among other things. I struggled in school at times, and I didn't know why at the time. I was misunderstood in this department at times. I would get yelled at for not understanding how to do certain subjects and having Cs and Ds on my report card. Actually, I would get yelled at a lot.

IT'S NOT ABOUT THE OUTWARD. IT'S ABOUT WHAT'S UNDERNEATH

It looked like I was just being lazy, but the truth is… I wasn't. I struggled. I would get told at times, out of frustration, "If you want to be nothing, then you go ahead!"

So many times, I wanted to yell, "I'm not being lazy! I need help!" But all I could do was cry.

The turmoil that I suffered from hearing these words and many other hurtful words began to take root in me. I didn't really have support in dating either. That's why I've only had two serious relationships in my entire life. I would hear things like, "Don't be no silly girl!" and "It's not you that I don't trust. It's them."

Not to mention, I didn't really see people in the church date either. It seemed like they just ended up married.

I wanted to experience what we call *normalcy* in different areas of my life, but unfortunately, during those years… I couldn't. I wasn't able to go to school dances (I did go to both of my proms, though), I couldn't talk about my high school crush or even have certain girl talks that I needed.

Back then, dating was off-limits, mainly because my mother didn't want me to experience anything that she was put through, and she didn't want me to fall into sin. I didn't understand that at the time; I just thought she was mean and strict. In actuality, it was her way of protecting me.

I saw emotional, mental, and physical abuse for a time while growing up. Even in my older years, I began to become scared and confused but wasn't quite sure how to articulate my feelings so… I did what most kids do, I kept quiet. I began to feel unloved. I didn't know how to channel my feelings. Who could I turn to? Where could I go?

However, there were some things that I did have support in and did receive love and compliments for, but was it enough to replace all the damage that was being cultivated in me?

How could God allow me to be in an environment as such? Would this be how my life would turn out? Would I repeat the things or be involved in the things that I experienced growing up later on in life?

My mother worked often, so there were a lot of things that I didn't get from her, but there were a lot of things that I did get. I have to say that my mother did try to support me the best that she could in my extracurricular activities. Growing up fatherless, for the most part, while only having my godfather around as a father figure for a short period, mixed with all these other things, put the conception of insecurity in me at a very young age. I didn't have the structure of a masculine authority around me, which made it difficult later on to really know how to respect men properly.

I walked around day in and day out, a very happy kid on the outside and some parts inside, but wishing my father was there. I had my older brothers, but that wasn't enough. My father was in jail most of my life growing up. I didn't get to see him at all when he was there, but I did talk to him from time to time, and he wrote me letters and would have pictures drawn for me and send them. My father was released from jail when I was in the fifth grade until I was in the seventh grade, and then he went back until I was thirty-one years old. I wanted to be able to see him, but it never worked out. He didn't want any of his family to see him there as he was, even though none of us cared about that.

During the very short time that my father was there, I would exaggerate the things that he would do for me. I felt like that would help me mask how I really felt and help me cope with the loss of time. It made me feel like a whole kid to some degree, and it helped to numb the pain when I exaggerated. I would be proud to say my dad did this or my dad did that. It made me feel like a normal kid. Later on in life, I accepted that gifts will never replace time.

I wanted both of my parents together at the time, but that would soon change. My mother wanted me to be the best that I could be growing up so badly that she was stricter about certain things than most. Also, it had a lot to do with the way religion molded her. At times, I felt that she became so righteous that she was no earthly good for me. I needed a mother, not an evangelist. I needed comfort and compassion, not condemnation and correction.

I endured some of the hurt that my mother carried from her upbringing. She would tell me stories, but I didn't fully understand

IT'S NOT ABOUT THE OUTWARD. IT'S ABOUT WHAT'S UNDERNEATH

them until I was an adult. My mother needed a mother. She longed for a mother. My grandmother was present but absent. She worked all the time, so one of my aunties was left to sort of *raise* my mother and her siblings. The anger my mother carried marinated in me while I was in her womb, but there was more than that.

As I grew up, I really started to learn who my mother really was. There were many times I would be exposed to her insecurities and other very real things about her that became too much for me to handle. I, later on, realized that some of the things my mother dealt with and carried became a part of me while she carried me. I would hear certain things from my mom, and I would become very angry and hurt because here she was, the one who was supposed to be my role model. The one who I needed to look up to would be the very one that I felt I had to break away from. How could I feel like that? She's my mother!

She was great at being spiritual and spiritually minded when I needed her to be, but I needed more than that. I used to wonder why she was the way that she was. My mother really didn't share her honest feelings about herself and her life with me until I was much older. I would only see and experience the effects of it.

This is why we have to remember that what we do today will affect our tomorrow.

As I continued to grow up, I had a very nice figure. There were a few who used to call me Ke-kola in high school because I had a Coca-Cola shape. I used to blush, but secretly I would be very excited if people noticed my shape. I felt important in a way other than just receiving the basic compliments that I was used to hearing. It made me feel attractive and noticed.

Guys started to show interest, but I eventually found out they only wanted me for one thing. I realized that they didn't care about *me*. They cared about themselves. Interestingly enough, for that reason, it made me resist. God's Word kept me. Although I had issues underneath that I masked, God's Word was rooted and was working without me knowing it.

The years went by, and I would wear a smile but become very angry inside. I was still such a sweetheart and as loving as could be.

Don't get me wrong. Those are real qualities that I possessed; however, there was another side to me that not many people knew. So now I had anger on top of insecurity.

I masked it very well. I was still going to church and being very active in church while living a what looked like a normal life on the outside—all while dealing with this thing that continued to evolve on the inside.

I would then come into a relationship at nineteen that would really spin me for a loop. I was in love, y'all! I felt so much peace and happiness during that time. I felt like I finally would receive the love that I had been looking for from mankind. My relationship seemed so perfect. Finally, someone who would accept me for me and who would sacrifice things for me that he normally wouldn't. He eventually got saved, and we did mighty work for the kingdom of God! I planted a seed, and it had a domino effect, and tons of young people were saved and filled with the Holy Ghost because of it! Families' lives were changed. Everything seemed so perfect…until… I messed up.

We both became weak, and even though I was stronger overall, I decided to give in and give away the very thing that kept me pure in one sense all these years. Now why did I do that? I immediately was convicted because what I knew to be true all these years from God's Word, keeping me struck me like never before. A sin that I abstained from finally got me.

Would God forgive me? Of course. God is so full of grace and mercy. I just didn't know how much at the time. Oh, but the consequences were very real! Things started to spiral downward and eventually came to an end. I felt like nobody would ever really love me the way that I needed. I really became insecure and angry after that. Not to mention, I felt so guilty. I carried guilt and shame for a very long time. Many will think this is small. However, when you know God's Word and live by it, it hits differently. Also, guilt looks different for everyone.

Think about a time when you may have been convicted of a thing or two or many. How did it make you feel?

IT'S NOT ABOUT THE OUTWARD. IT'S ABOUT WHAT'S UNDERNEATH

I made light of it and thought, *Oh, I'll get over it eventually. It's not that bad. I still had my friends and many other things that made me look great!*

However, all these *beautiful* outward things didn't hide the iniquity that had formed on the inside. God watched it all.

After my breakup with the person I was dating, everything slowly but surely began to come to a head. I became obviously angry, smart-mouthed, defensive, and many other things. I was so hurt and heartbroken. I didn't have my father, and now I lost someone who was near and dear to me.

At this point, I started to see and embrace the fact that I felt less than, unimportant, used, worthless, and many other things. I blamed myself. I was afraid to express my true feelings, so I held them in. I felt like I only had my two best friends and a few of my cousins at the time to turn to. Nobody else.

Some say time heals all wounds. Is that fact or fiction? Time eased my hurt but didn't remove it. I never even got the closure that I needed about it. There it was again. I was scared to speak out and didn't know how, so I just carried it.

I remember being at church one time, and the minister prayed for me. While fanning his towel at me, he kept saying, "Bless her to forgive. Bless her to forgive." He didn't know what I was dealing with, but God did.

That's when I knew it was time for me to start demasking and let God move me on, but how? I had to stop running. I had to stop being comfortable with who I thought was the *real* me and let God bring me to the *real* me. Who was I? I didn't know. I was about to step into a me that I'd never met.

I began to increase my faith the more that I heard God's Word, and I learned how to surrender to him.

Being raised in church from the age of three, I heard a lot of what we call sound doctrine, but that didn't stop the issues of life from flowing from my heart. I didn't really know what iniquity was until I was older.

When we don't take the time out and become honest and true with ourselves and God, we're blocking the healing that's waiting.

The true healing that only God can give. One day, I decided, after ten long years, to finally let go and let God. It was definitely a moment to remember.

Again, it's not about the outward; it's about what's underneath. How many times have you gone around masking things and situations that you know you needed to let go of?

It's so easy for us to *mask* things every single day of our lives, but is it beneficial? I know what it's like to say that's just how I am, but I want to say to you that is *not* how you are! We create all kinds of problems for ourselves, including physical problems, by not letting go and by not being willing to let God clean out the ashes that we see and the ones that we don't. It can't be done without honesty and humility. Let God give you beauty for your ashes. I know that it's hard, and I will not say that it'll be easy, but it will be *worth it*.

Take a minute and really think about that.

One day one of my sons had a wrinkled shirt on, and he tried to cover it up with a hoodie. I told him to iron his shirt, but he felt that he didn't need to because the messed-up thing that was hidden wouldn't be shown.

The only one who would know that his shirt was not in the best condition would be him. I told him that he still needed to iron it. Why? Because it's not about the outward; it's about what's underneath. Even in today's times where we literally wear masks, it's causing us to cover up. Cover up part of our faces, which may hide any physical flaws that we may have.

Others won't see, but we know it's there. When I decided to let God heal that part of me, that was only the beginning of my journey of letting him give me beauty for my ashes that were created. I know it's comfortable sometimes to sit in our space, not facing or dealing with the real secret things that stop us from moving forward and being who God truly created us to be.

I'm telling you, I've been there, done that, and I'm still coming out of things, but it is waaay better on the other side. No matter what you've done, have been through, and maybe are in, God's healing power is waiting to be bestowed upon you.

Identity

IDENTITY ISSUES ARE a thing that many of us have dealt with at one time or another. Even now, some may struggle. I remember being told that I had issues. Well, don't we all? Maybe I was struggling to find out who I was—just maybe. As I mentioned earlier, I had many things that I tried to identify with because I didn't know who I was.

Now I know that during teenage years and even young adult ages, we go through this thing called *trying to figure it out*. That's a little bit different from what I've experienced. I actually needed to figure it out. This terrible issue grew as I grew. I felt like I didn't fit in in many areas of my life.

In the church that I belonged to, at one time, I felt like there were places that I was being made to fit into and ways of operating that I had succumbed to. I struggled because I knew I didn't fit into that particular program. I would get irritated at times to be identified as a part of these things. I didn't want to be identified as such. I knew I had more in me that went above and beyond just this, but I wasn't sure how to access it or how to identify it.

When I was younger, I remember going through a tomboy stage. Not only was that the style, but I wanted to fit in. I picked up habits and traits and slang because that's who I wanted to be, but not really knowing that's not at all who I was. Who was Keke?

When I went through the phase of being angry and having a bad attitude, I started to identify myself as this person secretly.

Mainly because I received many complaints and judgments on those things instead of love, help, and support in the way that was really needed at the time.

When my mistakes started to arise, I had a problem with not seeing myself through those mistakes. I labeled myself by my mistakes, and the devil helped me do that. People helped me do that as well. Condemnation had settled in. God showed me how I looked at myself, even though I didn't know it at the time. I thought what I thought was right, but I was wrong—so very wrong.

I settled for things I shouldn't have settled for. I had thinking patterns that were beneath who God saw me as, and I had ways of operation of such. I was never taught the importance of learning who I was. For example, if someone is broke far beyond money, that's not who they are. They have the ability to find out who they really are and live in that.

On the other hand, if they don't choose to learn how to live out who they really are, then that'll be what they'll identify as, and others will identify them as that as well.

I started to feel like nothing more than what I would see in front of me, even though there was a small piece of me that knew I was more, but again, I didn't know how to access it.

I would try to navigate my way through the years with the hopes that the things that I desired would come to pass because I thought that may be it. I had a strong desire to be an actress. I've even done work in acting in Hollywood, and that's what I labeled myself as. I felt for years that I didn't want to be or do anything else. Was this who I was? Just an actress with nothing else to support her whole being? Was acting going to give me the identity that I was looking for? I have to admit, every time I was on a set, I felt like everything was how it should be. I felt like I was finally coming into the me that I had been trying to find—the me that I didn't know existed until one day, God said, "That's not it either."

What you do is not who you are. However, what you do can become who you are if you continually do it. That's why you have to watch what you do. It affects your character. There's a positive and a negative side to this.

IDENTITY

Many of us don't really know who we are, but we base it on what we're operating in. If all we do is work and go home, then that's who we label ourselves as and become just that.

There's another side to you. That's not all you are, so stop settling for the lack of in your life or the lower end of your life.

Growing up without proper teaching of the importance of learning who I am and learning the real importance of valuing myself, not just my private areas, I spent many years searching for the real me. Now of course, in my childhood, I was not going to worry about identity, right? I was a kid.

There was a time when I knew without a shadow of doubt what I wanted and what I didn't want, so to my knowledge, I thought that I knew who I was, but did I? I had values and standards that I held high, but then somehow, as I matured, I began to see the bigger picture.

The operation of my life had become clearer and clearer, and I was able to start seeing that maybe I didn't know who I was. People loved me so much and looked at me on the surface for the most part. I was innocent and sweet, and I was protected, or at least I thought that I was. The fact that I had identity issues didn't really show to others as it did to me.

It wasn't until I surpassed my teenage years and was very well into my young adult years that I started to realize that I really didn't know who I was. If I did, I wouldn't have settled for meaningless things and people that I allowed to be a part of my life. My standards would have been higher than they were.

I wouldn't have allowed myself to be treated in ways that were well underneath what I deserved from people and situations, but I did. If I knew better, I would've done better, but since I didn't, I didn't.

We struggle so much culturally trying to figure out who we are. Some of us research from generations and generations past as much as we can to find out who we are, and then there are some who are trying to find out who we are individually.

We must find out who we are so that we can execute our real lives. There are many opportunities that are waiting, but if you don't believe it, then you won't attain them.

I wore condemnation for many, many years. In some ways, I knew, and in some ways, I didn't know. I only lived with it. I used to beat myself up internally and wish day in and day out that I could turn back the hands of time to get away from the mistakes that were being pinned on me. The mistakes and foolish decisions would later cost me and wear on me like one of my favorite outfits. Condemnation presented itself, and I answered. All because I thought that I had to identify myself with that.

I didn't know myself as anything else that was solid and concrete that would give me the security that I needed. Yes, I was and still am a child of God, but did that stop me from dating condemnation? No, it didn't. I thought that I was supposed to be condemned, even though God clearly tells us that he does not condemn us when we are in him.

I let the devil make me think that I was someone I wasn't for far too long. He knew that I was blind, so it made it easier for him to deceive me. You will be in the wrong place, in the wrong position, in the wrong relationship, and many other things if you don't know who you are.

CHAPTER 3

Pride

PRIDE STOPS EVERYTHING. Pride is from insecurity and fear. We can have too much pride to admit that anything is wrong with us, and we can have too much pride in the sense of playing the victim all the time. Every time something happens, it's always everyone else but never us. Or it's always us doing everything (positive) and nobody else, and the way we vocalize it or our attitudes behind it show whether it's prideful or not.

Now we do experience things that leave us in a victimized state, but we don't have to stay there.

God *hates* pride. There are times when we walk in pride and may not even know it. There are other times when we know we have pride and can proudly admit it! If we let our pride down and cast our cares upon God, we'll see how much easier our lives will be in time.

The devil will use your circumstances to make you feel like you will forever be a victim to your circumstance, but I come to decree and declare that the devil is a liar! You can be made free and made whole by the power of the blood of Jesus! You are a victor!

In 1 Peter 5:7 (KJV), it says, "Casting all your care upon him; for he careth for you."

Whether you have a relationship with God or not, I know without a shadow of a doubt that he wants us all to be clean inside and out. How do I know? Simple. If he did it for me, I know that he can do it for you.

After I began my wonderful deliverance journey, little did I know that I would have another tremendous trial waiting for me. One that was much more tedious than the previous. More hurtful, more crushing, more humbling, and more victorious in the end. Apparently, I still had much more to be delivered from.

Many of the events that have taken place in my life have allowed me to wear a mask on and off. So I guess the saying is true, never judge a book by its cover. I've never been so close to that saying in my own life as much as I was during the tests and trials that I've faced to develop myself.

Wearing a mask can be an expression of pride because it hides the truth. In today's times, there are so many people frontin' on social media. It's ridiculous!

We don't want the real us to show, but that's who God wants to deal with and have a relationship with, not who we pretend to be. Sometimes, we try to front in front of God, but it's a waste of time because God can see right through us! He created us! We have to stop suppressing so much and receive the help that we need.

I know you may say that it's hard, and you don't know what I've been through, but God does. You may even cry your eyes out while doing it, or you may even need someone physically there to help walk you through this moment, and that's okay. Pushing through to bring beauty from the ashes out of an ugly situation doesn't always feel good.

People? Why do we front so much in front of people? A lesson that I had to learn. God really had to deliver me from people.

People can't add a day to our lives, nor can they add hair to our heads, yet we are so concerned with people. We size people up, and people size themselves up against us, but my question is why? *Pride*. That opens a door for so many other things: jealousy, boastfulness, and envy, just to name a few. Oh, and don't let us become busybodies in other people's matters! We have an opinion about this or that or feel like we have to be involved and always have something to say, but God is looking at us, asking things, like "What about this?" or "What about that?" in our own lives.

PRIDE

Pride is also a relationship killer. When we have actual relationships with people, and they're too prideful in them, it affects us. When there are arguments or disagreements, nobody wants to be the first to apologize, and it's hard for us to admit it at times when we're wrong. There are other times when nobody wants to talk about it at all, and the situation seriously needs to be discussed.

We're so concerned with what the other person did or didn't do. It takes humility to take the high road.

As I began to identify the areas of pride that I had and started to allow God to heal me, my heart started to feel different. Some things broke my heart but fixed my vision! I was able to see my flaws clearer, and I tried my best and am still trying my best to not wear any piece of pride. God showed me how ugly it is. I'm not perfect, but I'm working on it. So now if I happen to say or do something that pertains to pride, or when pride is in operation around me, I can identify it better.

I've been in many situations where I've been wronged or done wrong, and yes, I've had to bite my tongue and apologize. There were even times when we all knew that I didn't really do anything, but situations were manipulated, and I knew it, and still, I had to walk in love and apologize for the offense that I caused. Now I'm not saying let people walk all over you; I'm saying there are times when we have to be the bigger person. It's hard, but with the power of God, it can be done.

That's why we need God's strength because we, in our human form, alone can't possess certain strengths that are needed. I had to pick up my Bible and create a prayer lifestyle if I wanted God to move me. If I didn't know his Word, I couldn't stand on it and allow it to give me strength. If it was one scripture, I let that scripture take root until I gained enough strength to allow it to start operating in my life.

How do we walk in humility and not in pride? The first thing to do is to admit. Admit to God the truth. It's only us and God. He's not going to go and tell his disciples what we did (joke); he already knows, but he wants us to come to him with the truth. It's about relationship.

I've seen many people feel like their bragging and boasting aren't prideful; they're just excited. What I mean to say is that, for instance, when God blesses us in an enormous way with something we've worked so hard to attain or something we've waited so long for, we have a tendency to get puffed up. When what *we* did starts to settle in and we start receiving all these compliments and things like that, that's when the devil can easily slip into our thoughts. We may say to ourselves or even out loud, "Yeah. I did that!" And we somehow slowly put God on the back burner and forget that *he's* the one who did that! If it wasn't for him, we wouldn't have or even have the desire to have the things that we do.

Now I'm not saying compliments aren't nice, and to feel good about what we've accomplished is wrong. I'm saying that in our hearts, we must always remember that without *God*, nothing is possible, and we need people to see what God has done through us and for us.

Forgiveness

FORGIVENESS IS A very hard thing to do. I mean true forgiveness. Are there any people in your life that you haven't forgiven? Do you need to forgive yourself? If so, ask yourself, "Why haven't I forgiven this person or this situation or myself?"

True forgiveness takes time. I'm not talking about reconciliation; I'm talking about forgiveness. They're two different things.

Many times, we think forgiveness goes hand in hand with reconciliation, and that's just not true. It's another lesson I had to learn. Forgiveness was for me, not them. I always thought it meant that once I forgave, then I had to reconcile, and in turn, I think that made me struggle with forgiveness.

Sometimes, it's not healthy to be reconciled with the individuals or situations. Boundaries need to be in place. If I know someone is a manipulator or an abuser or a user even, and I fall victim to one of these situations, I can learn from it and forgive them, but it may not be wise to reconcile the relationship with them *unless* they've proven that they've repented and changed. Even then, reconciliation still may not be an option. It may be that the relationship is over. No hard feelings; it's just over.

When we understand this principle, it helps save us from getting into cycles of toxicity. I remember taking a nap one day years ago, and while I was asleep, I saw this bright light behind a face that I needed to forgive. The light was so powerful, and I remember cringing in my sleep because of the intensity. I literally felt like something was being burned out of me. God was killing the unforgiveness toward that person that I carried.

When I woke up, I felt so refreshed! I felt so clean, and that's because God had healed me, which enabled me to have the power to forgive all at once! I never looked back at that situation ever again. I needed closure. God gave it to me.

When we forgive, we take back the power that was stolen from us. Forgiveness was a weak area for me, and that's why God kept letting me get into situations—tough situations where it required me to forgive. God wanted to shed light on and perfect that part of me.

I remember it being so easy to have evil thoughts toward people who wronged me. Thank you, Lord, for having mercy on me! Geesh! You would never think. Yeah…little ol' me. Again, I was masking my true feelings. I didn't let it appear how I truly felt.

In order to be right with God in any kind of way, we *must* forgive. In fact, the Bible tells us that if we do not forgive, our Father in heaven will not forgive us. Why not? We wrong him every day of our lives. We can't expect to wrong God and get forgiveness and then have someone wrong us and not forgive them.

God called us to be whole human beings, not broken and damaged. He wants us to know in full what he created us to be. I know that there are areas in your life where you need to forgive. Don't let pride stop you from making that step.

God is waiting for you to come and receive all the healing and other blessings he has waiting that you haven't even seen yet.

King David had to forgive Saul for trying to kill him. Just think if he didn't. Would he have lost his position? Maybe. God called King David because he knew what he had underneath. His heart was pure for God.

When the prophet Samuel went to anoint David as king, God told him not to look at the outer appearance. Man looks at the outer appearance, but God looks at our hearts!

David didn't have the *look*, but he had what was underneath!

I knew that if I didn't forgive all those wonderful people who wronged me, I would be blocking myself from moving to the next level of what God really had for me. I used to think that I forgave people because I wasn't angry anymore. That was a smooth deception to get me to move on, but I did it broken and did not know it.

It hurts at times to have to truly forgive. I remember wondering how I could be the one with the *bad end of the stick*, while everyone else walked around appearing perfectly fine. I actually didn't have the bad end of the stick. God was trying to develop me so that he could move me forward.

God showed me what humility looked like in forgiveness. It was hard. I have to admit. There were times I wanted to go off on some of the people who had wronged me while in my forgiveness process. I've had to turn the other cheek. Despite suffering embarrassment and what I felt was shame, I still had to forgive and ended up treating them cordially with a peaceful heart. All while I knew some thought that I was to blame, and while some thought that they were better than me, in reality, I believe that they were secretly jealous of me—not so much of me but of the way God made me and of the spirit that he gave me. Many have shaken me but could never break me! They've tried. I've been accused falsely, had lies spread, embarrassed, neglected, belittled, rejected, dealt with abuse after abuse, and then some. All by the people who were supposed to love me. People who I never thought of because they were supposed to love and protect me but failed. Some failed in certain areas, and some just failed.

One of the churches that I used to belong to really was a pure foundation for me to exercise forgiveness. I used to feel like a black sheep at times, although many used to portray that they loved and supported me. To be hurt by the people that you've helped so much is a very hurtful thing. I was shunned in certain ways because it made others feel better about themselves, and I didn't understand it at first. All I could see was me being treated unfairly. False accusations about me went on secretly from time to time, and the thing that really got me was: why didn't anyone ever approach me?

I would have to hear about it from people who didn't have an issue with me. I tried to follow what the Word says about settling differences, but they didn't know how to do the same. I got tired. I would see people minister the Word but then know them on a different level. I would see how the Word was manipulated, but I felt that I couldn't say anything in love. I would be looked at as little ol' Keke. That's how many looked at me for years.

I played a very vital role, and you would think that I would've had a lot more support than what I did. The support I received appeared real, but then, as time went on, people's real hearts began to show. The thing that really bothered me was how much gossip went on. I mean, it was ridiculous!

People watched me walk around hurt and didn't say or do anything about it. They acted like it wasn't even there, but then there were those few who really had my back.

How can you say that you love God and preach and act so saved but won't even extend your compassion to someone that you know was hurting and that was done wrong? I never understood it.

Whispers and gossip are what I survived through for many years. I watched secret messes unfold in many situations. It was crazy! The church is supposed to be a place of healing, comfort, deliverance, and so much more. I did experience those things. However, I experienced many opposites. Control issues started to rise, pride started to rise, and sin crept in, and here I was thinking that people I was around with really had my back when, really, they were involved in other messy situations.

Time went on, and I felt like I was the only one who understood those who were crying out for certain things but not receiving the help that they needed.

I would be told by the ministerial staff, "Oh, it's this or that." Things that would not be edifying to the believer but would tear them down in a way. I went to them out of concern and in the hopes that we could work together to try and help.

One time I was having an issue, and I reached out to one of the leaders. I was really hurt, and I explained what was going on, and they told me in a very harsh voice that what I was going through was my punishment for a past action that put me in that position. That was not the way to handle that! I was looking for help, but instead, I was torn down! That pushed me away from ever going to them with serious issues again.

From that point on, I never wanted to share anything personal ever again, and I just watched many others begin to fall into the same trap that I did.

I started to get angry because nothing was working anymore. I began dreading going to that particular church. It was never supposed to end up the way that it did.

Where was God? Was he in that? No, but he was sitting back the whole time, watching and waiting to move. Things changed, but not for the better. It got worse to the point where I started feeling suffocated. I couldn't do it anymore. One day, I became fed up because many parts of my life had become strained. I finally decided to do something about it. Enough was enough. A time came when I left and never looked back.

After I was freed from that part of the bondage that I was in, God reminded me of something. God reminded me that I was worth saving. I heard it loud and clear. God came to remind me about Jesus, the one who died for all our sins. After not really being able to embrace his grace in many areas, he came to remind me that it was still there. For a long time, I had developed a thinking pattern that didn't include God's grace and mercy to a certain degree.

What is mercy? Mercy is when God knows how messed up we are, yet he still loves and wants a continual relationship with us. Mercy is when God still calls us and wants to use us, even though we don't deserve it.

Grace is when God is still wanting to perform the plans that he has for our lives regardless of our past.

God forgives us, but one of the hardest people to forgive is ourselves. I struggled with forgiving myself for a really long time. I possibly somehow began to have resentment toward myself. Things that had been over for quite some time, I would still feel guilty about. I knew God had forgiven me, but there was this thing called condemnation that would pop up from the devil that would make me feel like crap.

God had a remedy for it. He told me there is, therefore, *now* no condemnation to them that are in Christ Jesus. Wait huh? So you mean to tell me that I don't have to walk around feeling guilty and ashamed and crappy because I'm in Christ Jesus? Absolutely! Those who don't walk after the flesh but walk after Christ's spirit? Yes!

I was gettin' played, and the devil knew that. He was playin' on my emotions by making me rehearse my past and relive certain moments in my head. I wasn't exercising the word that I needed that's in God's Word. I would pick up my Bible and pray about other things, but not forgiving myself. I would have people tell me that I needed to forgive myself, but honestly, at the time, I didn't think it was that bad, so I kind of took it lightly. I was deceiving myself.

It wasn't until I had a serious conversation with my mother one day, and God opened my eyes through her. From that point on, I started taking heed to the Scripture, and I let it take hold of me. I wanted to move on. I wanted to be free.

All I can say is God. All this was a part of him preparing me for the beauty that was waiting for me.

CHAPTER 5

What You Do Today Will Affect Your Tomorrow

WE MAKE SO many decisions from day to day. At times, we don't think about it; we just do it. Is it done by faith, or is it done by not using wisdom? We've had many conversations about our physical appearance, and oftentimes we're compared to our mother, father, or siblings. What about our personalities? The way we think, the way we behave, and the way we speak.

Think about the word *generational*. We use it a lot, and even the Bible talks about generations countless times. Adam and Eve sinned, and here we are, generations later, paying for it. Adam was made a tiller of the ground because he was stripped of his job of maintaining the garden of Eden and having authority over it.

He then started to have kids. One of his sons, whose name was Cain, automatically became a tiller of the ground as his job. Why? Well, because of his parents' disobedience. Cain developed a heart with evil in it. As a matter of fact, it was so evil that he became jealous of his brother and killed him! That was the first murder of humanity.

God was furious with Cain, and he definitely punished Cain. Now let me be clear, God is still and always has been and always will be a loving God. However, everything we do in this life has consequences, good or bad. You reap what you sow.

So now Cain went from being a tiller of the ground to not being able to grow crops at all. He was left to be a restless wanderer on the earth. Generations later, Cain had a great-great-grandson. He goes on to tell his daughters-in-law that he killed *two* people. He said if God avenged Cain seven times, then God was going to do it to him seventy-seven times!

Do you see how things were passed down generationally? What we do today will affect our tomorrow! What are we passing down? What has been passed down to us? For me, once I started to mature and learn about really where I come from and who I am, I had to be honest. There were some things that I didn't like. Did I have to be stuck with it because it ran in my family? *Absolutely not!*

Once I began to understand more, I came to a point where I wanted to break what we call *generational curses* over my life because I no longer wanted to operate in them, and I sure didn't want my kids to have it. You don't have to settle for "Well, my momma did it," or "My daddy did it," or "My grandma and whoever else."

You can turn it around and become a *victor*, not operate as a victim. When we hear or have heard things like "You're just like your mom or dad," is that a good thing? We must figure that out, so we can know whether it's a compliment or something that needs to be dealt with. Now there are positive generational things that I've inherited, and you too. These are what we call generational blessings.

Abraham, in the Bible, was able to pass down generational blessings. He was a man of *faith* and *wealth*! God blessed him to pass down those blessings through his generations.

As my children got older, I started to see more things in them that had been inherited, and my eyes and ears are becoming more and more sensitive to these things because I know where they came from, even though they may not fully understand them. This is one reason I fight so hard to train and raise them in certain ways because there are things that need to be broken, and there are things that need to be developed.

As I mentioned earlier, decisions are vital to our everyday lives. We must be careful about the decisions that we make because it does affect our tomorrow. How many times have we said, "If I would've thought," "If I would've been more careful," or "If I would've listened?" Why? Because when the consequences come, they're not always what we want.

More so, it affects others. How many broken families do we have because of fulfilling our lustful desires with one another? And then there you go—another human life is at stake. At stake of not having Daddy or Mommy around, not having a real example of what family really is, or having a family that is toxic. These are just some of the consequences of the decisions that we made at that time. Now I'm not saying that God can't or doesn't restore because he has blessed many to live in the grace and mercy of blessings in that area.

Thank God for that! When he beautifies, he does it well!

The consequences of the past actions that I've made turned into ashes because once I realized the seriousness of it all, it became that much harder to deal with. The pain burned so bad that it turned into ashes.

When I first got pregnant with my first child, I went through hell—not just physically but spiritually as well. I panicked initially and even considered abortion (even though I knew I wasn't really going to do it), but a mother at my church at the time looked at me one day and said, "Don't do it. It's going to be a part of your testimony."

I was blown away, and I knew that was God speaking to me because I had never shared with her my thoughts on this! Boy, oh boy, was she right! I would later come to find out how right she was. I made the biggest mistake of getting involved with their father at the wrong time, and I paid dearly for it. God warned me, but I didn't listen.

I knew better. God was trying to protect me because he saw what was up ahead. I was young and inexperienced in many areas. My image got tainted for a little while. I had an image that I turned to love secretly, and it all became ruined in my eyes. I knew that I wanted children, but not the way that it started. There's a scripture that says a good name is better than riches. I wanted my name to be clean again.

I admit that when I first found out I was pregnant, I was mortified. I wanted to run, but where to? I didn't know much about generational curses and blessings at that time. I didn't know that my daughter would someday take on emotions that were almost identical to mine in certain areas.

In the beginning, I didn't have the support from my mother that I needed or wanted. That was a feeling that I never thought I would experience. Why was that? Could it have been that she saw herself all over again and didn't want to voice it? Possibly, because what you do today will affect your tomorrow.

I rushed and got married because I thought that I knew what I was doing. I partially felt pressured by some people who were supposed to be guiding me spiritually. People who were supposed to look out for me and teach me how to follow God's voice. I believed at the time that they could hear from God better than me, so I trusted in the guidance that was being given to me. I'm sure you can tell by now how strong my faith is.

What really hurts is that my own mother didn't even give me congratulations when I told her that I was engaged. I felt so small and useless. This was one of the major moments in a person's life—not having support from your parents during this moment is one of the most hurtful things in the world. I understood later on where my mother came from, though.

Pregnant out of wedlock and then getting married to someone that I don't even really know. Way to go, Ke! I got engaged when I was six months pregnant. Not because I was pregnant, but because I thought that he was the one. Did we give it time? *No.* Did we know each other like I thought we did? *No.* It was just messed up all the way around, but it didn't seem as bad as it was at the time.

Time went on, and my mother eventually came around. She began to accept my new life and began to let God heal her from the hurt that I caused her. She began to forgive me and turned into the support that I always needed. God really gave me back the time that I felt was lost. Now I can't separate her from my family! I've come to really see that she may be quiet, but the power of *God* inside of her is not! I wouldn't trade her for the world.

WHAT YOU DO TODAY WILL AFFECT YOUR TOMORROW

Now because we thought we were ready to get married at the time when God was clearly telling us to wait, our marriage suffered down through the years, and eventually, it affected our children in many ways. I suffered a lot in my marriage—more than what anyone knows.

My marriage became a mess, and some people knew it but never gave me the proper help that was needed, especially when they knew they could've. I knew that God would eventually turn it all around for the good, even though it was very, very hard to see. I knew because his Word tells us that.

I had people who were secretly jealous of what they saw but didn't know what I dealt with behind closed doors. Beautiful outwardly but a total mess that would later turn into a message years later. One baby after another, unplanned, and being that was already a mess. That just added to my marriage. Yet I tried to stay strong. I tried to be the way that I *thought* God would want me to be. What a religious mindset I carried.

Little did I know that my perception of God was slightly off because of certain things that were taught to me. I thought if I divorced, I would be single with all these kids. Why? Because God takes covenants very, very seriously, and he knew that I knew better. It was my job to make it work. Although God does allow divorce in some cases, these were my thoughts. Especially after constantly being told nobody's gonna want you, I started to believe that.

I entertained manipulation for quite some time and didn't know it.

Nothing was going right. I didn't have the wedding that I truly wanted, nor did I have the marriage that I dreamed of. I had someone tell me once, "You need to look in the mirror and say you was just stupid!" and continued to tear me down instead of being there when I needed it.

This is why it's important to have a real relationship with God so that we can follow his voice. I didn't know God back then like I thought I did. When you listen to God, he knows how to *stop* you from making unnecessary mistakes—mistakes that will leave you broke, busted, and disgusted. Yet despite all that, he knows how to give you beauty for ashes.

Think of something that you've done or something that happened to you that affected you later in a very serious way. Even in my sin, God still had grace and mercy on me. God allowed me to suffer some things because there are always consequences for actions. He used it to shape me and mold me, and he didn't let guilt take over my life. The devil wanted to destroy me with shame and guilt, but God saw my future, and he knew that I was going to need some concrete strength for where he was taking me.

I look back on all the things that I've been through, and I no longer regret them because I learned from them. It matured me, and most of all, God gets the glory out of all my tests, trials, and tribulations. I'm taking every lesson that I've experienced and the ones that I experience now and applying them to my life.

I'm a better parent because of it, and I'm an overall better woman because of it. I look at wiser ways on how to deal with my children and life in general because of it. What I do today will affect my tomorrow. I'm doing my best, with God's help, to break the generational curses that run in my family.

I refuse for my children and future grandchildren to deal with things that were put in motion to destroy their lives by generations past. *Generational curses shall be broken!* We don't always have to have things modeled in front of us to repeat things that run in our family. Interesting, to say the least. However, many of us need to really know where we come from.

A lot of us have hidden things that nobody wants to talk about in our families because we've learned how to be silent. Molestation is happening, and we're silent. Abuse is happening, and we're silent. Manipulation is happening, and we're silent, and there's so much more. We become silent and move on from day to day while burying this hurt and detriment in our hearts. We learn to wear a mask.

We never get healed at the root, and then we have children. Our children inherit our character traits, whether it's from us or our parents or generations past. Then we have the nerve to get angry at our children's behavior when they act it out. If we don't know where we come from, we won't know how to deal when we see things come out in our children, and we won't really know the truth about ourselves.

What you do today will affect your tomorrow. The anger problem that I had came from more than just the things that I went through. It started to show, and it was ugly. Someone once said to me, "I've never seen a young person just so unhappy," and the way that it was said hurt me because it was as if they were disgusted with me.

Years later, as I began to learn more about my family line, I saw that anger was one of the things that I inherited. I got reprimanded and scolded and misunderstood a lot for being this way, and due to me not knowing my family history, I thought that it was my fault. My parents both dealt with anger, but somehow I was expected to not have anger issues.

I was expected to not deal with some of the things that were passed down to me. Ummm, yeah right. God watched everything. One day, he said enough is enough! I stopped running from the healing that I needed. I got desperate for healing. I got tired of my life being a mess. I got tired of wearing a mask. I got tired.

You have to want change in order for change to happen. God is waiting to heal and reveal the truth to you, just like he did for me. God wants to make you whole. The Bible says that the thief cometh not but to steal, kill, and destroy, but Jesus said that he came so that we can have life and have it more abundantly. What does *abundantly* mean?

"Plentiful," "much." We need to stop existing and really start living. It doesn't matter how much material things or money we have. You can have all that and still be broken. You can *look* like you're doing good because you *made it out of the hood* or because *you're successful outwardly* and still be messed up.

God kept showing me for a long time that I was being robbed. The devil was robbing me—robbing me of my peace, my joy, and my confidence. When I finally identified what or who the devil was using to do those things, I rose up. I had to start taking back what *God* said that I could have.

I don't want that for you. You don't deserve to live like that. Look at all the things or people that have robbed you and left you in pieces. If nobody has ever told you that you're worth more than your mistakes or your circumstance, that you do have a purpose, and that you *do matter*, I'm telling you! It's not too late to change the direction of your life so that the thing that's keeping you from being whole and abundant doesn't continue in your life or your legacy!

In the little time that my father was around, I saw the kind of relationship he and my mother had. Little did I know that years later, I would end up dealing with similar things. There was a time when I felt like I didn't need my father. I felt like I was okay and that my mother was really all I needed until I got hurt from my first relationship and when I started suffering in my marriage.

I wanted to blame my father for not being there and not teaching me things regarding relationships from a man's perspective, or should I say, showing me how a man is supposed to treat a woman. It was hard because I only had what my mother was able to give me. Was that enough? At times, it wasn't.

The expression "Knowledge is power" is very true. Had I had more knowledge in certain areas, then I would've had more power to exercise wiser decisions. However, experience is your best teacher. Because of the things that I've been through, I've become more and more passionate about helping others to really consider their actions before taking them. Really consider the effects that they may have down the line.

I know that there are many who wear the statement, "If I only knew back then what I know now," or "I wish I could do it over." Yeah, that was me for many, many years.

Then there are some of us who say, "Oh well, the damage is done." Even if that's true, how are you moving forward from it?

Are you moving forward in pain, bitterness, and unforgiveness but masking it by acting like everything is okay?

My marriage suffered for many years because there were two people with many, many masked issues. There were a lot of hurts, pains, and insecurities. I thought that I was ready to be a wife when I got married, but the truth is… I wasn't. I was excited about this new chapter in my life, even though I had a couple of people tell me that I didn't *have to marry him*.

They spoke from a place of them thinking I was getting married just because we had a child. *Wrong!* I thought this was God giving me someone according to his will for my life. To be quite honest, he wasn't my ideal at first. However, I called myself moving in what I thought was faith. Faith in my future. Faith in God's plan that he knew fully of, but I didn't.

At the time, my spiritual state was young. I mean, I wasn't a stranger to God, but I thought I knew God better than what I actually did. During that time, according to the way that I was taught, I believed that God put people together for ministry purposes ultimately and not really anything else.

You see, God does things with purpose. If he blesses your marriage, it's for the fullness of it, not just certain parts of it.

What I mean is, I don't believe God will allow you to get married *just* for ministry purposes or just so you can legally lie in bed together, etc. At the time, I thought it was only limited to ministry in the church building. Ministry has so many avenues and is *not* limited to a church building. That type of ministry, as well as others, can be birthed out of the union, and his and her ministries will work hand in hand. However, your family is your first ministry. Marriage was designed *first* to be an expression of the relationship between God and the church. God loves us so much. This is why God is so serious about marriage. Marriage is supposed to be a beautiful thing.

I've heard the scripture that it's "better to marry than to burn" used several times. So much to the point where the understanding that I had was if you couldn't contain yourself, you'd better get married. Regardless if you were deeply in love with the other person or not or whether you were ready or not. I lived with this understanding for many years until I started to really seek God for myself and get understanding from *him*.

During these times, my praying and studying were elevated like never before, and I didn't stop until I got the understanding that I needed. God started to allow my spirit to be disturbed by this understanding because he wanted me to seek him for the truth.

There are specifics in the Bible for husbands and wives to go by. God commands husbands to love their wives as Christ loves the church—so much that he gave himself for it. Okay, Christ died on the cross for each and every one of us. That is sacrificial love, and that's how husbands are supposed to be with their wives. I'm not saying to die literally, but die to your flesh, die to your pride, and die to your selfishness. Die to many other things that will cause a drift between husbands and wives.

Those are the kinds of sacrifices husbands and wives ought to make. Wives are supposed to be treated delicately; however, we have to submit. Wives must submit to their own husbands. Submission doesn't mean being a doormat. I used to think that's what it meant because of the incorrect teaching of the Word, and I looked at my marriage. I thought cooking, cleaning, and being in the bedroom whenever he wanted was submission, regardless of how I felt or was being treated.

That's slavery, not submission.

I came to correct that! *Submission* is me trusting my husband enough and *choosing* to lay down my will and let his will lead us according to what God has given him, and there is agreement. It's a choice. However, we, as wives, have to feel safe, cared for, secure, and loved enough to do this. Now let me be clear; I'm not talking about losing ourselves. I'm saying that I'm trusting the vision that he has for our marriage and family and that we will end up prosperous because his ear should be in God's mouth. I had a very hard time with this area, and then I got to a point where I stopped. I got tired of being treated the way that I was and of being this ugly young woman on the inside.

Obviously, God's way wasn't in operation. I cried many nights, lost weight at one point, and had hair loss so much because of stress that I had to cut my hair into this *cute* pixie cut. My marriage became emotionally and mentally abusive. I wasn't always perfect, either. In fact, I may have been worse than I thought. I became stuck—stuck in more than one way. I was going back and forth between my mom's house and my house, unsure if I should divorce or choose to believe that the devil had inserted himself directly in the middle of my marriage, so I should stay and fight. I had children. I needed to make sure that I was present continually in my children's lives. I hated for them to see me taking them back and forth every so often from their grandma's house to our own house because of the poison at home.

So as the years went by, many more things transpired. We eventually stopped doing a lot of things to keep our marriage alive. My marriage began to die. It was still unauthentically beautiful on the outside but very burnt up and contained many ashes on the inside from the fire going out. We ended up just existing and not living—not living the abundant life that Jesus had for us. Was it hard to maintain decency in front of our children? Yes. Were they hurt by some things? Yes.

Some of you may ask why I stayed this long or why I didn't divorce. Well, I had some fear and uncertainty. Again, I became stuck. I was a housewife for fourteen years, and I didn't have anything to land my feet on. I feared that I would lose my children, and I also had some misconceptions about divorce according to the Scriptures, which would give me the mindset of not wanting any more consequences. This is why we have to study and pray and ask God ourselves about his Word. We need teachers as well but don't solely rely on them.

I lived in such a dark place for a long time, and those who were close to me hated it. People began to know my business more than I expected, and so I felt like the spotlight for gossip and negativity was on my marriage. I was grateful for the support that I did have because there were many, many times I wanted to give up. As a matter of fact, some parts of me did give up. I felt like some parts of me had died.

I hated seeing my children unhappy, but I refused to leave them because I didn't want a fight that I thought would eat me up and leave me helpless.

I felt inadequate, worthless, used, abused, unloved (again), and many more things. How could I come back from that? Every time we got separated, to me, it seemed like God always brought us back together.

There were plenty of times I thought, *Okay, now we're really about to work this out.*

Nope. Only to find out we were ending up like the children of Israel going around in a circle. We needed to get to the root of things, which seemed so hard to do. You see, when God heals, he heals at the root! That's what we needed terribly.

I began living beneath what God would have me to live. I started having my faith challenged in my life. I started to question if God even really cared about my situation because I would read his Word but not see it manifested in my life. We tried counseling several times, but nothing seemed to work, yet God kept telling me that my miracle was on the way. I lost big pieces of myself and didn't see how or when I could get them back. I was losing my identity.

God continued to minister to me, and he sent ministers to me without them knowing it to help carry me through, and I actually had a small support system as well, but I still felt alone. Now I used to wonder how it was that God kept giving me something to look forward to, but nothing seemed to be happening. Was I imagining things?

I started to settle with my life being the way that it was—broken, busted, and disgusted with five children at this time. I was embarrassed and ashamed on the inside and didn't really see a way out until one day when I really got tired. I was tired of my life being the way that it was, and I became determined to do something about it! I gave up trying to hold on and continuing to go in the direction that I was going in.

I was ready to let it all go. I didn't have any more fight in me.

I started to meditate on Jeremiah 29:11, which tells us that God knows the plans that he has for us, plans of good and not evil, to give us hope and a future. I always loved this scripture, but I didn't apply it to my life as I should've. As I started to read over this scripture, I began to declare this over my life, and then something happened.

God said "Enough is enough!" God spoke the word *divorce* to me as clear as day, and the other word he gave me was *comfort zone*. I carefully meditated on the things that were coming before me, and I was on my way to the divorce court.

I had to go back to the beginning of my marriage and confess and cry out to God from the pit of my heart that I messed up. I had to repent. I had to take the mask off and be raw and real with God. I had to repent for how we got together and for letting other people manipulate me to go against what I know God told me. I had to repent for not keeping God at the center of my marriage and allowing other things to come in and take his place. I repented a long time ago, but not like this. I was willing to throw everything away just to show God that I was serious about repentance.

The further I got into my preparation, I heard God say wait. I was like, huh? I've been waiting. I'm finally free, and now I have to wait. You see, when God speaks, it's far more deeper than we know. During this time, God began to reveal more truth about things to me. The truth that would later reveal itself in the natural. So as I was waiting, God explained what he meant by *divorce* at that time. God was telling me to get up and arise and take my rightful place! To walk in the authority that he has given me and stop letting the devil run my life. God cared about healing me before dealing with my situation.

Divorce all the hurt, shame, and guilt because Jesus already died for all those things! Divorce that false teaching that would keep me in a mindset of bondage! Divorce those false agreements that would ruin my life! Divorce depression! Divorce spiritual suicide! Divorce all those things that are not like *God*! The devil tried to kill me!

Oh, but *Jesus* said that he came so that we might have life and have it more abundantly! God wanted to deliver me! I had to separate myself from my marriage so that God could build me back up the way that he wanted me to be so that I could live out the life that he has called me to so that I could let his light shine through me and so that I could fulfill the purpose that he has set before me!

I was so dim, and I wouldn't be of any good to anyone at that time. Oh, but when *God* does it, he does it! So as I began to change and shift, my household didn't understand it because God was doing a *new* thing in me. They didn't understand who this new person was. I began to talk differently, and I began to move differently. God began to shift my atmosphere according to his Spirit through me.

You want to see change? Invite God into your situation! I let God be number *one* in my life again, and I wanted to do things his way. God began to give me strength and boldness about the direction that I was headed in. God kept leading me to focus on the assignment that he gave me.

It took me a while to figure out what that was, and then he finally let me see that it was my children. Focus on bringing them up according to the way he would have me do it.

That's my first ministry, my family, and I left my husband to him. He told me as clear as day to move out of the way, so I did.

God was bringing me into the life that he had created specifically for me. I started to remember that I had a purpose and that I had a destiny to fulfill.

At that point, I wasn't worried about anything or anyone. I mean that in the sense that if you're with me, you're with me, and if you're not, then you're not. It felt good because my life hasn't always been like that. When you stand still and begin to grow by letting God handle your situations, everything else that is not supposed to be there will fall off. There were many times, while enduring these rough and challenging moments, that I did worry, even while moving in faith according to what God was saying to me. I worried sometimes.

I've always had an issue with worry. I was worried about what others thought of me so much, worried about how this or that would work out, and worried about whether people liked me or not. I put so much into identifying myself through the lenses of others. If this one thought it was good, then I knew I'd be okay. Or if that one wasn't mad at me, then I knew I wouldn't have any problems at that time with that person. I'm telling you guys, I was so messed up. People were my biggest thing. I always wanted everyone to like me and accept me.

Why did I care so much? That's another sign of insecurity. Could I possibly have put so much energy into giving people that space in my mind that I somehow made them a god? An idol? When you put more time, effort, and energy into something than you do the Almighty God, then you have created a god other than the one and only true God. I was looking for people to fill that empty space with security. I know it probably sounds strange to a certain degree, but it's the truth. This was actually how broken I was.

It Takes Two, but It Starts with One

IN THE GARDEN of Eden, Eve was deceived by the devil, which caused her to disobey God and set a tone for generations to come that would affect us today. It took her to agree with the devil, which would make her sin. It started with one, but it took two. As I look back over my life, I've made a few agreements that never should've been made.

The agreements that I made turned into lessons. When I agreed in the past while thinking what I was doing was small, it actually wasn't. The person who was affected the most was me. Why? Because I knew better. Many of us have made agreements that will be with us down the line. Be careful with what and whom you agree with.

What about when God makes agreements with us? It starts with one, but it takes two. When I began to come to agreement with God, my life started changing for the better. When I wasn't in agreement with God, I found myself doing things on my own, working harder than I should, and going through things that I shouldn't have.

I was immature and thought that my way was the best. My actions showed my immaturity. My blindness, if you will. The Bible says that "there is a way that seemeth right to a man, but the end thereof is death."

When we come to agreement with God, we come to agreement with safety, comfort, and blessings that we didn't even know were there! When we come to agreement with the devil or our own righteousness, we come to agreement with deception, lies, false hopes, and pretty painted pictures with a big hole behind them.

When you have a relationship, it starts with one, but it takes two to make the relationship work, and I'm talking about a relationship of any kind. Too many times, especially in today's times, we see one-sided relationships. I was in a one-sided marriage in many areas for a long time.

There are many of us that carry the weight of things, and it's supposed to be distributed equally. I heard many stories about the workforce being unfair, for example. There's always someone not doing their part, which causes one or many to suffer because of it.

When there's no agreement, then purpose can't be born. When God makes an agreement with us, he always keeps his promise! It may take some time, and it may look like it'll never happen, but that's not true! If God said it, it's going to happen! I used to get very discouraged and anxious and allow doubt to come into my mind when it came to the things I desired for God to do in my life.

I used to say, "I know he can, but I don't think he will."

This is the lens that I used to look at God through. I believe that I developed that because of how many men have not kept their agreements with me throughout the years and let me down. Somehow, I subconsciously looked at God like that.

I used to fear God in the wrong way. I used to fear God in the way that if I made a sinful mistake, that would be a mark against me. I had the mindset that I'd go to the lake of fire if I kept allowing myself to fall into sinful situations, even though I was trying to be right. I later came to know that God wasn't like that.

When he tells us to fear him, he wants us to revere him.

Little did I know that God was hurting, longing, and waiting for me to agree and come into real a relationship with him. I was not practicing religion, which I was very good at one point. I wanted a relationship with God, but because of my young understanding, I wasn't doing it how it really ought to be done. God is nothing like man at all.

I know some will probably wonder how you can come into agreement with God for your life. It starts with humility, admitting that you need him in your life. I had many situations that caused my life to have a fire that would turn into ashes, but God was creating beauty the entire time. I couldn't see how or even have the understanding to know that beauty would come out of my life to the degree that it has.

While my life was set on fire and waiting to be blown out, I was being refined. It took me to agree with the proposer, which was God, for him to blow out the fire. The fire burned so long that there was a lot of ashes. God had a plan the entire time to give me beauty for my ashes. Although I did things against God, without God, and away from God, he's so good that he would say, "I see all those ashes that are waiting to come from that fire, but I'm going to take them and still give you beauty and still make you into what I've created you to be before you were in your mother's womb!"

When I knew God was calling me higher and closer to him, I had to eventually stop running. What are you running from that you need to come to an agreement with what will further your life or make it better?

I ran and fought when God called me to certain people, places, and things. One main reason is confidence. I wasn't confident enough to walk in the direction that he was calling me to.

There are many times when we are just a decision away from taking that next step. It starts with the mind to agree or no longer agree that will bring change. I stopped agreeing with the things that were no longer serving me and that would stop me from being the best version of myself. It started with one, me. The more that I said *no* to the devil and my own self-sabotaging thoughts and began to say *yes* to God, I began to see miracles happen in my life!

I'm telling you again that if God did it for me, he can do it for you! One changed mindset will change everything, but when will you stop being scared to change your mind? God is waiting to do his part in your life because he has and is doing it for me. What are some things that you need to agree or disagree with?

I wanted the atmosphere in my household to shift to the way that I wanted it. I wasn't the best version of myself. As a matter of fact, I didn't like who I was for a long time. I felt defeated, and I didn't know how. I was scared to come to an agreement with God and to let him do it his way. I didn't know what that would look like or where I would end up. I had so many questions and worries with so little answers.

I would hear so much about how God can do this or wants to do that and how I was this or that. It was really hard for me to believe and receive those words for my life. Many of the things that I was told, I couldn't see. I didn't see how God could lift me up, clean me up, and set my feet in a position for the atmosphere to shift.

I wanted it to happen the way I thought it should go. There's a saying that if you want to make God laugh, tell him your plans.

I was very traditional in my thinking. While knowing God operates outside of any box and that he could never be put in a box, I somehow thought my way was right. I couldn't comprehend why God wasn't allowing things to happen in the order that I prayed for and the order that I thought things were supposed to go in. All these things were stopping me from stepping out in faith and coming to an agreement with God.

I'm going to be honest. I couldn't stand to hear people tell me sometimes that it's me that God wanted to change or that he may not change my situation, but he would change me. I couldn't stand it because I ran from it. This is how we are when we hear the truth about a matter but aren't ready to receive it. I wanted my situation in my marriage to change. I wanted out.

I even told people once before at my church at the time, while we were separated, not to talk to me about it. I didn't want them to encourage me to believe in God to fix things opposite of the way that I wanted them to be fixed. I was so messed up.

You see, that's just it. God doesn't operate in the way we think he should all the time. Little did I know that God was waiting to make me laugh. I spent so much time misunderstanding and feeling angry and running that I felt like I wasted a lot of time, but God doesn't waste anything.

None of my tears were wasted; none of my tests and trials were wasted, but God used them for his glory and for the development of me! Why do we hold on to things that are actually weights in our lives? We make excuses as to why we continue in toxicity, whether it's in relationships or whether we carry the toxic trait ourselves. God is calling us out of all the mess that we wear and live in every day. God is calling us to an agreement with him.

I finally accepted and allowed God to fix *me*! When I finally surrendered and let God do what he wanted to do with my life, I was finally able to take the mask off. I no longer had to walk around feeling defeated, faithless, and scared.

If we would just come to an agreement with God in our lives, whether it be to make a change or whether it be to accept his offer of forgiveness and love, and allow him to be the head of our lives. I mean it truly, not lip service. I finally made that step to come to an agreement with God so that his glory could shine in my life.

There are many people who struggle and who are stuck that need deliverance. I needed deliverance, all while having a relationship with God. God promised me in his Word that he would deliver me out of all my troubles, and I began to stand firm on that, and I began to believe it. The more that I heard the Word, my faith began to build, and that allowed me to eventually put action to it.

I had to make a conscious decision to move forward with my life, as I stated earlier, and that's when God began to move! I came out of agreement with the things that are not of God and made up my mind not to go back to the old way. When we do things before we're ready or when our sincerity about them is not there, we tend to go back. Why go back to the vomit that you threw up?

What I'm saying is that when God wipes you clean, brings you out, and gives you what you've been praying for, *don't go back! Keep moving forward!*

I know I was scared at one point of letting God heal me. I didn't know what that would look or feel like. I was comfortable with where I was, and sin was attached to it. Why was that when I knew that being in the state that I was in wasn't taking me anywhere?

We've all heard the expression, "You have to take the first step." God took the first step in extending his hand for me to come into his presence so that I could receive the healing that I needed, and all I had to do was agree. It takes two, but it starts with one. I've been in the same place as Eve a couple of times before. I allowed things or people to deceive me. They did it well too, but I thank God because he revealed the situation and exposed the evil-doer!

God would speak to me in dream after dream and give me songs with messages about moving forward. Scriptures would stand out to me, and I would know that it was God. When I started to accept and embrace the things that God was presenting to me, it was then that I was truly able to start my road to the emotional healing that was waiting for me.

God told me that he was going to do a *new* thing in me, but I didn't see it for years. I would testify and preach about *new things*, all while still trying to understand how and what he was going to do with my life. I remember living in Bakersfield, California, and I was one of the speakers for a service that we were having.

Several years prior to that, God had introduced me to the fact that he was going to do something new in my life. I believe it was 2012. There's a scripture in Isaiah 43:19 that says, "Look, I'm doing a new thing! Do you not see it?" That's one scripture that wouldn't leave me. However, at that time, my response was… No, I didn't see it.

I looked for years for God to perform what he said, but things only got worse…or so it seemed. I had to hold on to the Word, though. So when Bakersfield came in 2013, I let this word about new things fall dormant in my heart but still tried to be obedient to what I believed God wanted from me.

It was very hard because I was unhappy, felt undervalued, and many other things. I always knew God knew better, though. So as I started to study what God would have me speak about, the scripture came up again. Everyone received the word that was brought forth! However, I still found myself looking for that to manifest in my own life.

All these things God was speaking to me about helped me keep pushing. Brokenness, weakness, unhappiness, anger, and worthlessness—just to name a few—are what I carried throughout many years. I wasn't in agreement with God, although I thought I was. God doesn't think any of these things about me, and neither does he think these things about you!

IT TAKES TWO, BUT IT STARTS WITH ONE

I cried and cried and prayed and prayed, but I still had this stinking thinking. The more I prayed and became open from being tired of being out of agreement with God, the more he came in, which allowed him to start the cleanup process! I always knew that I had something in me that needed to come out.

Comfort Zone

COMFORT ZONES CAN be tricky. It could either be a blessing or a detriment. Well, in my case, it almost became a detriment. It was November 2019 when God started speaking to me about my comfort zones. He gave me the illustration of how he told Abraham to get out of his country and his kin so that he could be shown something much greater. Imagine having to leave everything you know—everything that is structured and concrete for something God wants to show you.

I began to look at my life and surroundings, and I started to understand more and more of what God was talking about. The thing is that God didn't speak to me once. He spoke to me multiple times, and each time, my understanding grew. I finally got to the point where I started believing that I was really going somewhere—somewhere fast.

It was then that I started separating myself from anything that wasn't like God. God revealed to me that my comfort was in how I was living, which was beneath who he wanted me to be. My comfort hindered me from letting God's light shine through me because I was full of things that were not benefiting me.

Many times, when we've become complacent, it blocks us from moving forward. I thought my life would be no more than what I was looking at, although God clearly tells us that he has a plan for

COMFORT ZONE

us to prosper. Well, was I prospering? It certainly didn't feel like it inside. Maybe that's why God told me to get out of my comfort zone.

God has put too much in you for you *not* to walk out of the benefits that he has for your life and for you to live the abundantly blessed life that he called you to! Living a blessed life doesn't have anything to do with material things. It's time to stop thinking that we're blessed because of what we have primarily. Blessed is who you are first!

In order to access the fullness of what God has, comfort has to be dismissed. I was comfortable but not happy. Too often, we are comfortable with things that are not benefiting us, whether seen or unseen.

It was time for me to switch to a different state. A different state of mind because I couldn't go to the next level and experience the next level of beauty with how I was.

There was a huge part of my life that I hadn't seen yet! I either had to stay stuck in how my life was going or say I was done!

I'd seen comfortability modeled in front of me growing up. In fact, I saw comfortability run through my family. Comfortability in lifestyles that would later become real-life struggles. I never thought that I would find myself attached to comfort, which would be a downfall for me, but I did.

I wasn't intentionally attached, but it was something that developed. We don't always like comfortability, but we are still able to engage with it very well.

I can remember previous times when God was trying to take me to another level. He would show me that I was in a comfort zone. We can never elevate without being dismissed from what's familiar. Faith takes us away from familiarity and comfortability. Just think: when we elevate on the job or venture out on a new path in life, we leave what's comfortable.

Yes, it can be scary, but it's so rewarding! When we take flights, for instance, we leave the ground level and elevate to the top. We leave what's comfortable. When will you leave what's comfortable to walk on another level that God has for you? You may not feel like you have anywhere to go to, but I can guarantee that you do.

We all have places, people, and things that we have yet to still come into contact with that will push us to our next step. God showed me that there would be consequences if I didn't leave my comfort zone, and the consequences would be that I wouldn't receive the blessings from the level that he was trying to take me to and that I wouldn't reach the people that were waiting on me.

Why not? Just like when we need something from the store, we have to go and get it. We have to exercise our mobility and go. Same thing here. God is saying to exercise your faith and go get it!

You may be sitting and wondering how you can get out of or get unstuck from where you are. I'm here to tell you that God is waiting for you to make the first move! He's already done his part, and what he promises is real! God is a promise keeper! When we delight ourselves in him, meaning when he takes pleasure in us, he will give us the desires of our hearts!

Faith moves God! Some of you already have desires that God put there, but you don't know how to begin to walk in them. Baby steps with consistency. That's how I started. Once I understood that I was comfortable being uncomfortable, I wanted to change. I started changing the way that I thought and continued to pray for God's hand to keep holding mine. I listened to messages and inspirational things to help me keep moving forward. The resources that I needed, God provided.

Over time, I became stronger, and I had support around me to help me stay encouraged. Support is a necessity! It could be family, close friends, counselors, therapists, or whoever. We need it, with God being our ultimate help!

I support you! I want to see you prosper, and I want you to live the fullness of the life that God has for you! I may never see you in this life, but my prayers can go further than I ever could! So can yours!

Think about who's dependent on you. God wants to make you the next trendsetter! God wants to make you the example, and you can do it only if you move in faith and *push*! I know all about pushing a little too well—I have six kids! I pushed out every last one of them!

COMFORT ZONE

I was comfortable until it was time to be uncomfortable. I was comfortable until I was in labor. It was time for things to shift. It was time for me to birth something and move to another level! It was time for the next phase of my life that God had already written for me!

It was the same situation when God wanted me to move away from my comfort zone. Earlier, I mentioned divorcing my state of being, which was ultimately killing my call. I became comfortable with my stinking thinking, my unhappiness, and everything that I thought about myself that was opposite of what God thought of me.

I was going to die in my comfort of being uncomfortable and not knowing or accessing the other side that God had waiting for me. It was scary to let go and try something new. I had forgotten what it would feel like to let go and let God at this particular time.

I had experienced it before, but this was different and a lot more comfortable because I had been in it so long. The longer we stay comfortable in a thing, the deeper we go and the harder it is to get out. God had to remind me that he is the same God yesterday, today, and forevermore, so what he did for me before, he was waiting to do it again. I didn't know how to let him do it, though. I didn't know how to let God heal me. I didn't know how to stand up for myself and not care about what would happen to me after.

Vulnerability can be a very scary and difficult thing, especially when we've had so many traumas or disappointments in our lives. We create a pocket for comfort and a wall of protection. It's easier to run away from healing, or whatever it is that we need, and becoming uncomfortable to take us to an unseen place for our benefit.

It's easy to say, "I don't want to talk about it."

It's easy to shut down or abandon the things that need addressing.

I had insecurities that I used to try to hide because it would be uncomfortable to say or show what I lacked. I didn't know at the time that God wanted to move that out of the way so that he could show me what he really equipped me with and that I could.

God wanted to expose the devil that had a hold of my mind and how he continued to make me comfortable in hiding. He wanted to expose the devil and how he wanted to keep me feeling like I couldn't when God already said that I could!

I had to be vulnerable, and I knew that it could possibly hurt. It hurt to let go of all the emotional turmoil and belief that my finances would stay just as they were. It would hurt to believe again. Just like in surgery, when the wound heals, it gets hurt in the same spot again, and the doctors have to go back in and operate again.

It hurts, but I had to push through in order to be better. I made up my mind because what did I really have to lose? Especially when I felt like I had lost a lot already. I no longer wanted to hide. I no longer wanted to have surface peace and healing. I wanted the real thing.

Think about hoarders. They hoard everything, and they are comfortable! If we'll be honest, some of our lives are like that. We hoard things. We hoard bitterness, loneliness, envy, jealousy, pride, ego, hurt, disappointment, lack of love, insecurity, and many other things, and we've become comfortable. These things will block your blessings and the freedom that God has for you! You'll go about your daily lives broken, busted, and disgusted, and you'll carry these internally as if this is your plight. Live as if you're not being weighed down by these things. You live with it and have settled with it.

Well, I'm telling you that you don't have to live like that! It's time for the devil and all life's setbacks to get back! It's time for you to start walking in your deliverance and freedom! God promised it to you, and you have every right to possess it!

There's so much fakery going on in the world today. We hear the words "She's fake," "He's fake," or "They're fake" all the time. Have we ever thought about the why, though? Could it be that they've become comfortable being fake because they were so determined to not deal with the root cause? I mean, think about it. Some of us are fake because we are not totally happy with ourselves inside or out, but there are other reasons we do it. Some will read this and say, "Oh, I know I'm not fake, but you might be comfortable being openly bitter."

Where does this come from?

Could it be that it's a learned behavior? If I had not been careful, I would've allowed the little bit of fronting that I was doing or the fakeness that I was holding to become a part of me more than it did.

When I decided to go for it, I first admitted to myself and to God the truth, being willing to risk everything else that I had left and trying to be obedient to what I knew he wanted for me. That's when he stepped in.

God began to turn everything around. I was focused on the things that he put in front of me, and I was consistent with it. God saw it and began to bless the little that I had, and slowly but surely, he began to multiply them. I gave him my ashes, and he began to give me beauty.

Beauty for Ashes

ONE DAY, A friend of mine was putting on a youth conference, and she asked me to be one of the speakers. At this time, I didn't really feel adequate, but at the same time, I felt honored. I knew that God would bring me before people to share what he has done for me. I just didn't know how or when. So when she asked me, I actually was elated on the surface but nervous, as I didn't know what was on the inside.

What would I speak about? I was still waiting for certain testimonies to come to fruition. I was tired of sharing the same testimony over and over, although people were blessed by it. I thought to myself, *God, what should I do?*

So God gave me this scripture, Isaiah 60:3, and it talks about how God will give you beauty for ashes and the oil of joy for mourning. There's an exchange going on. As I began to read this scripture and meditate on it, I started to reflect on all the things that I've been through.

God was telling me right here in his Word that if I would just give him all my mess, he would exchange it for something better. God had been trying to tell me this all along, little by little, but I didn't fully understand that.

This scripture would be the testimony of my life up until this point. At first, I thought that it would have only applied to one circumstance that I had gone through, but God was extending it. I had to wait until I came out of it to be able to see.

The more I applied my faith to this scripture and allowed God to work it in my life, I was able to see that God was doing this the entire time. He was molding me and making me into something that he would call beautiful, and I didn't even know it. I used to feel like God had forsaken me because the pain of producing beauty hurt so bad.

God wanted glory out of my life, and he wants glory out of yours too. I had to go through the refining process, just like when diamonds are refined. They're refined in the fire until they get to how the creator wants them to be. It's hard but oh so rewarding. There are many great things in store for you, and you must go through the refining process. To receive the beauty that God wants to give you, you have to let him do all the work in you. I know it may seem scary, but you won't ever regret it.

I've been through so much in my life. I went from being a people-pleaser, angry, in despair at times, rejected, living in unnecessary cycles, hurt, sharp-tongued, having no hope, feeling like I had no future, and then some to meeting God, who turned it all around!

There was a time in my life when I wasn't able to help anyone. I didn't know how. That wasn't even on my radar to do it according to how God called me to do it. I wasn't there yet. I had to get past God. Where are you? First. I never thought God would change my name from insecure to secure and from brokenhearted to full of love. Only God can do work like this.

I went from being ashamed to being unashamed. God did a total 180-degree turn with me.

God is a healer, a deliverer, my redeemer, and so much more! I didn't just get over my problems or randomly find a new way of thinking about them. Absolutely not. The power of God came in and cleaned me up, washed me up, and made me new! Made me whole! There's a certain type of healing that only God can give. He gets down to the parts that are deep enough to get hurt but too sensitive to let anyone touch them. I used to be scared of deliverance and healing until, one day, I accepted God's invitation to let him come in and visit me in a way that I had never seen. I can tell you my redeemer lives. God lives in me, and he wants to live in you. Live in those dark areas. Let him shed some light on them.

God is waiting to make you into what he already sees you as. He's the help that you've been waiting for, searching for, crying out for, and praying for. I'm a living witness to what God has done and will do. I used to say I know God can, but I don't think he'll do it for me. That was where my faith was, and I didn't know it at the time.

I came to let you know that thinking like that is not from God. The devil will keep thoughts like that in your head to keep you from receiving what God has waiting for you. We like to say, "What if it doesn't?"

But now it's time to change to "What if it does?"

You are valuable and loved. You do have a purpose. You weren't brought into this world by accident. God designed you with a strategic purpose in mind, and he's waiting for you to live it out. God will make a way out of no way for you, just as he's done for me. All the ashes that you've been carrying, it's time to do an exchange. Give God a try for yourself, and let him blow your mind.

You may not understand your purpose or define your purpose by the things that you've been through, but there's a greater purpose, and God will use those things to help bring you the beauty that he's waiting to give you. There's a whole life that's waiting for you that you haven't seen yet.

When God begins to give you beauty for your ashes, it's like a refreshing wind or a refreshing drink of water that runs from deep within, and it's untouchable. Nobody can shake or change what God has done once he does it. They may try, but it won't work. Walk confidently in it continuously and guard what he's given you.

I can honestly now say that I'm living my best life, and it has nothing to do with what material things I have or have access to. It has nothing to do with the type of career that I may have, but it has everything to do with what God has done for me.

God has lit a fire in me that will forever burn and will continue to get stronger and burn more fervently as I go in and out of each day. The fire in me burns from the inside out, and it's as bright as the sun on a warm, beautiful day. This fire feels amazing.

I understand beauty differently now. Beauty is more than just skin. Beauty is what God brings out of ugly situations, and beauty is what God saw in you and me from the beginning of time. Just as an artist puts a bunch of art together and calls it a masterpiece, which is beautiful to them, that's what God sees in all of us.

So again, I ask, "Will you let God give you beauty for your ashes?

ABOUT THE AUTHOR

KEISHANDRA SMITH IS a mom, a speaker with a prophetic voice in the community, and she has a passion to help others live out the life that God has for them. Over the years, she has learned that God can take the lives of people and turn them beautiful, no matter how ashy they may be. Her ability to connect with people from all walks of life has prepared the way for her journey.

The California native's writing journey began when she was just a teen. However, in her older years, she took the road of background acting for a while. She's done plays and even appeared in a Netflix series. Going through life's experiences took her back to writing. Little did she know that it would turn her into a published author. You can find her as Keke Smith on Facebook and as @iamkekesmith on Instagram.

Printed in the USA
CPSIA information can be obtained
at www.ICGtesting.com
LVHW041648180823
755494LV00003BA/661